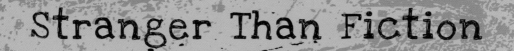

Stranger Than Fiction

ODD INVENTIONS

By Virginia Loh-Hagan

Disclaimer: This series focuses on the strangest of the strange. Have fun reading about strange people and things! But please do not try any of the antics in this book. Be safe and smart!

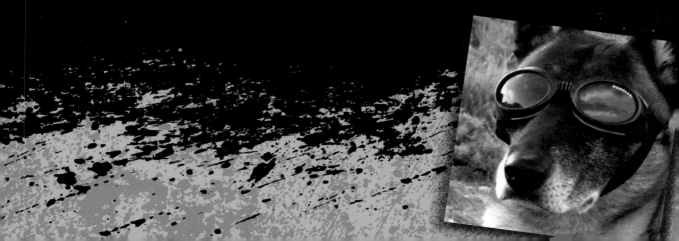

45th Parallel Press

Published in the United States of America by Cherry Lake Publishing
Ann Arbor, Michigan
www.cherrylakepublishing.com

Reading Adviser: Marla Conn MS, Ed., Literacy specialist, Read-Ability, Inc.
Book Designer: Melinda Millward

Photo Credits: © Falcon1708/Dreamstime.com, cover; © The U.S. Army/http://www.flickr.com/ CC BY-SA 2.0, 1, 14; © den-belitsky/Thinkstock, 5; © Masterchief_Productions/Shutterstock.com, 6; © Al Freni/The LIFE Images Collection/Getty Images, 7; © Nicola Bertolini/Shutterstock.com, 8; © mammuth/iStockphoto, 10; © Dreef/iStockphoto, 11; © Bettmann/Getty Images, 13, 25; © Falcon1708/Dreamstime.com, 15; © meunierd/Shutterstock.com, 16; © North Carolina Museum of History, 17; © Tony Crescibene/http://www.flickr.com/ CC BY-SA 2.0, 18; © Jeff Baumgart/Shutterstock.com, 19; © David Pereiras/Shutterstock.com, 20; © Miyuki Satake/Thinkstock, 22; © Kues/Shutterstock.com, 23; © CraigRJD/iStockphoto, 24; © CamiloTorres/iStockphoto, 26; © Les Gibbon/Alamy Stock Photo, 27; © CHAjAMP/Shutterstock.com, 29; © StockCube/Shutterstock.com, 30

Graphic Element Credits: ©saki80/Shutterstock.com, back cover, front cover, multiple interior pages; ©queezz/Shutterstock.com, back cover, front cover, multiple interior pages; ©Ursa Major/Shutterstock.com, front cover, multiple interior pages; ©Zilu8/Shutterstock.com, multiple interior pages

45th Parallel Press is an imprint of Cherry Lake Publishing.

Library of Congress Cataloging-in-Publication Data

Names: Loh-Hagan, Virginia, author.
Title: Odd inventions / by Virginia Loh-Hagan.
Description: Ann Arbor, MI : Cherry Lake Publishing, [2017] | Series: Stranger than fiction | Audience: Grades 4 to 6. |
    Includes bibliographical references and index.
Identifiers: LCCN 2017001054| ISBN 9781634728911 (hardcover) | ISBN 9781534100695 (pbk.) |
    ISBN 9781634729802 (pdf) | ISBN 9781534101586 (hosted ebook)
Subjects: LCSH: Inventions—History—Juvenile literature. | Inventors—Juvenile literature.
Classification: LCC T48 .L64 2017 | DDC 609—dc23
LC record available at https://lccn.loc.gov/2017001054

Printed in the United States of America
Corporate Graphics

About the Author

Dr. Virginia Loh-Hagan is an author, university professor, former classroom teacher, and curriculum designer. She invents stories and ways to scare her husband. She lives in San Diego with her very tall husband and very naughty dogs. To learn more about her, visit www.virginialoh.com.

Table of Contents

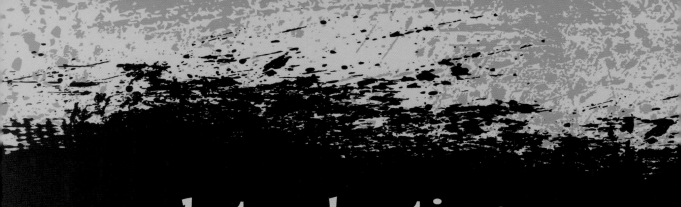

Introduction

People are inventing all the time. They make new things. They come up with new ideas. They build on current ideas.

People invent for different reasons. They see problems. They want to solve problems. They want to help people. They want to improve the world. They want to make things easier. They enjoy creating.

Some inventions are useless. They don't make sense. They're strange. But there are strange inventions. And then, there are really strange inventions. These inventions are so strange that they're hard to believe. They sound like fiction. But these stories are all true!

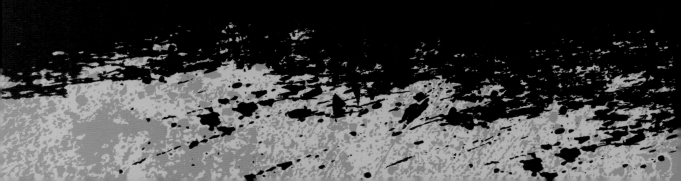

One of the first human inventions was fire.

chapter one

Pet Rocks

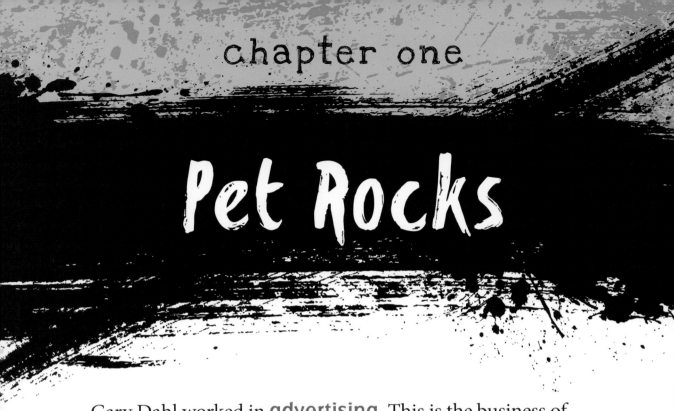

Gary Dahl worked in **advertising**. This is the business of promoting things. He invented pet rocks in 1975. He was in a restaurant. His friends complained about their pets. This gave Dahl the idea.

People told him it was dumb. But he didn't listen. He said rocks weren't just rocks. He said they were pets. He said they were the best pets. He said they were easy to care for. Rocks didn't need to be fed. They didn't need to be walked. They wouldn't die.

He packed the rocks in cute boxes. The boxes were **carriers**. Carriers are special

Pet rocks were a fad. They were popular and then died out.

pet containers. They had handles. They had air holes. They had hay beds inside. This kept pet rocks warm. It kept them comfortable.

Each pet rock came with a book. The book was a **manual**. It gave instructions. Its title was, *The Care and Training of Your Pet Rock*. It had many jokes.

People loved this idea. Pet rocks were a huge hit. Dahl sold 1.5 million pet rocks. He did this in the first six months. Each rock cost $3.95. Dahl made $3.00. He spent one penny on rocks. He found smooth rocks. He got them from Rosarito Beach. This is in Mexico.

It was easy to teach pet rocks to "sit" or "stay."

8

Explained by Science

Inventors practice trial and error. They learn by doing. This is a science idea. They make things. They try things out. They make mistakes. They learn from mistakes. They try again. They work to get things right. Edward L. Thorndike was a psychologist. He studied how cats acted. He made puzzle boxes. He put cats inside. He watched them try to escape. At first, cats took a long time. But they kept trying. They made fewer mistakes. They escaped by pulling cords. They escaped by pushing poles. They escaped more often. They escaped more quickly. Thorndike noticed the law of effect. He said successful behaviors tend to be repeated. He said failures tend not to be repeated.

chapter two

Blizzard Cones

Blizzards are snowstorms. Blizzard Cones were invented in Montreal. This is in Canada. This happened in 1939.

Women wanted to protect their makeup. Windy days messed up their faces. So did rainy days. They strapped Blizzard Cones to their heads. The cones covered their faces. They were clear cones. They were made of plastic.

It didn't work. Women would breathe. This made the cone fog up. Women couldn't see. Their cones got hot.

It can get really cold and stormy in Canada.

Women would sweat. This messed up their makeup anyway. It was also hard for them to talk.

chapter three

Goofybike

Charles Steinlauf invented the Goofybike. He did this in 1939. His bike was really strange. It had two levels. It carried four people. It even carried a sewing machine.

Steinlauf steered from the top. He used a car steering wheel. He pedaled with his son. His son sat in the back. He was on the bottom level. Steinlauf's wife hung off the side. She had a table. She worked on a sewing machine. Steinlauf's daughter sat at the front. She sat on the handlebars. She didn't do anything. The legs of the sewing machine came out. This was how the bike rested. This stopped it from tipping over.

Steinlauf created the bike for his whole family.

chapter four

Doggles

Doggles are dog goggles. They're sunglasses for dogs. They're tinted. They fit the shape of a dog's head. They make dogs look cool. They protect dogs' eyes. Some Doggles have special lenses. They help dogs see better.

Roni Di Lullo invented them. She has a dog. She saw him **squinting** in the sun. Squinting means partly closing the eyes to see something. She wanted to help him. This happened in 1997.

Many military dogs used Doggles. Doggles were sent to Iraq. They kept sand out of

14

Doggles keep dogs' eyes from drying out.

dogs' eyes. Di Lullo said, "Doggles were worn by the dog who helped find Osama bin Laden."

chapter five

Self-Kicking Machine

Tom Haywood built a self-kicking machine. He did this in 1937. The machine kicked people. It kicked them in their rear end.

The machine had a wheel. The wheel had four **spokes**. Spokes are thin rods in a wheel. Each spoke had a shoe. People would bend over. They turned a crank. This moved the wheel. People got kicked.

Haywood did stupid things sometimes. He needed a kick in the pants. This helped him be good. Haywood kept the machine at his store. His store was by a

CROATAN - 10 Miles East of NEW BERN, N.C.

Have you ever said "I want to kick Myself"? Heres your Chance

The self-kicking machine was a roadside attraction.

major highway. Many people used the machine. Some
people think Lucille Ball used it.

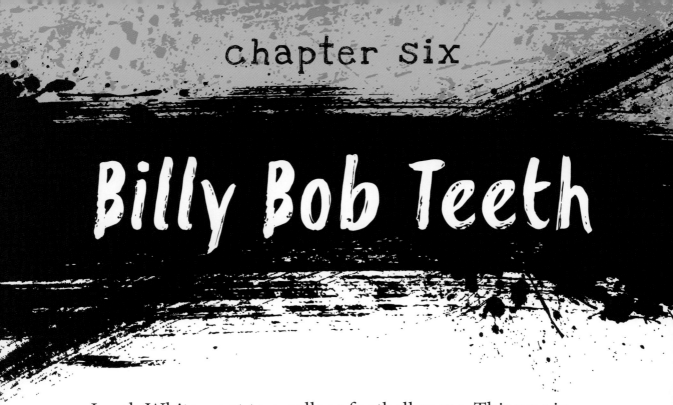

chapter six

Billy Bob Teeth

Jonah White went to a college football game. This was in 1994. He saw Rich Bailey. Bailey made people laugh. He wore fake teeth. He was learning to be a dentist.

White was curious about the teeth. He wanted to know how they were made. Bailey gave White a lab coat. He snuck him into his school's lab. They made fake teeth. They made 6,000 pairs. They sold them at state fairs.

Billy Bob teeth work like a mouth guard. People slip them on. Gums look like they're rotting. Some teeth look like they're falling out. They look strange.

Over 20 million Billy Bob teeth have been sold.

White created a business. It's called Billy Bob **Products**.
Products are things that are sold. Bailey became a dentist.
He left the business. But White kept at it.

His business is doing well. He got famous. He made fake teeth for movie stars. He made Austin Powers's teeth. Austin Powers is a funny movie character. Miley Cyrus is a singer. She wore Billy Bob teeth. They teamed up. This increased sales.

White wore Billy Bob teeth for his identity cards. He said people couldn't tell they were fake.

He had his own TV show. The show was called *Billy Bob's Gags to Riches*. Gags are jokes.

White's business makes over 250 different gag gifts.

Spotlight Biography

Kiowa Kavovit is a kid inventor. She invented Boo Boo Goo. Boo Boo Goo is a special bandage. It's like water. It's rolled on the skin. It won't peel off. It won't let water in. It doesn't make trash. It comes in different colors. Kavovit was 4 years old when she invented it. She looked at her knee. She saw a Band-Aid. She talked to her father. She said, "Daddy, what if I had skin that I could paint on?" They made Boo Boo Goo. She was on *Shark Tank*. It's a TV show. People pitch ideas. They try to get money to start businesses. She was 6 years old. She was the youngest person on it. She won.

chapter Seven

Toilet Briefcases

Niban Too is a Japanese business. It invented a special **briefcase**. A briefcase is a small suitcase. It's for papers. Businessmen have them.

The Gotta Go Briefcase has a toilet. It saves businessmen time. Busy people don't have to find a bathroom. They can open up their briefcases. They can pee in it. They can poop in it.

The briefcase is made of leather. It has a stainless steel toilet bowl. It has a toilet paper roll. It has a privacy panel. It can hold 175 pounds (79 kilograms).

The toilet briefcase is waterproof.

Fancy briefcases also have cup holders. They have hand soap. They have mirrors.

chapter eight

Dimple Makers

Isabella Gilbert lived in New York. She invented a machine. It was called a **dimple** maker. She did this in 1936. Dimples are dents in people's cheeks.

The dimple maker was a wire frame. It fit over a person's ears and chin. Wearers turned two knobs. The knobs cut into their cheeks. It was painful.

People were told to use it a lot. They wore it at night. When they woke up, they'd have "a fine set of dimples." The machine didn't work. Doctors didn't like the dimple

People used to do silly things to try to improve their looks.

maker. They thought it was unsafe. They said it might make people sick.

chapter nine

Gerbil Shirts

Gerbils are small, furry animals. Some people keep them as pets. People want to be close to their pets. So, someone invented gerbil shirts. This happened in 1999.

Gerbil shirts were vests. They had plastic gerbil tubes. The tubes ran all over. They wrapped around the chest area. The tubes' insides had grip. This let gerbils move better. The tubes had air holes. This let gerbils breathe.

Gerbil shirts were easy to clean. Owners could run a hose through the tubes. But the shirts could be dangerous. Owners couldn't fall. This would panic the gerbils.

Gerbils are very social. They like living with other gerbils.

Gerbil pants were also invented. But they weren't popular.

chapter ten

Fart Filters

Everyone farts. People eat. Air gets trapped. It's trapped in our guts. It needs to come out. People burp. People fart. This keeps people healthy.

Some scientists say people fart six to 20 times a day. Farts can make sounds. They can smell. This is embarrassing. So, a company invented fart **filters**. Filters mean to remove something unwanted.

Fart filters are like stickers. They can be put on underwear. They're a special cloth. They're made from charcoal. These filters **offset** smelly gas. This means they cancel out smells.

People don't know if farts are going to smell or not.

People wear tight underwear. This is so farts can't escape. They stick on fart filters. They keep knees together. This lets farts escape through filters. They stand with legs together. They fart slowly.

29

Paul O'Leary is British. He had gas problems. He invented Shreddies. This is special underwear. British soldiers inspired the name. They marched a lot. They'd shred their underwear. O'Leary sewed fart filters into underwear.

Ancient Egyptians used charcoal filters. They treated bad smells coming from wounds. Filters were used to clean water. This started in the 18th century. Today, we use them to hide stinky farts.

The filter cloths have been used in chemical warfare suits.

Try This!

- Think of a problem. Find a way to solve it. Invent something!

- Host an invention contest. Tell friends to solve a problem. Give them a time frame. Host an event. Let people share their inventions. Choose the best invention. Give out awards.

- Create an inventors' club. Meet on a regular basis. Share your progress. Give each other suggestions. Share ideas. Support each other.

- Learn more about science. Learn more about engineering. Take classes.

- Talk to an inventor. Ask questions about their inventions. Ask questions about their process.

- Collect five things from your house. Challenge yourself. Invent something using those things!

Consider This!

Take a Position! Inventors get patents. Patents protect their rights. They don't let others steal or copy their ideas. Some people think ideas can't be owned. Some think patents discourage creativity. Are patents necessary or not? Argue your point with reasons and evidence.

Say What? What is your favorite invention? Explain the invention. Explain why you like it. Include the inventor. Include how it was invented. Include what the invention does.

Think About It! Not all inventions are good. Do some research. What are some inventions that did not help humankind? How did they do more harm than good? How can they be changed to be more helpful?

Learn More!

- Editors of Time for Kids Magazine. *Everything Inventions.* New York: Time for Kids, 2015.
- National Geographic Kids. *125 Cool Inventions: Supersmart Machines and Wacky Gadgets You Never Knew You Wanted*! Washington, DC: National Geographic Kids, 2015.
- Turner, Tracey, Andrea Mills, and Clive Gifford. *100 Inventions That Made History: Brilliant Breakthroughs That Shaped Our World.* New York: DK Publishing, 2014.
- Wulffson, Don, and Laurie Keller (illustrator). *Toys! Amazing Stories Behind Some Great Inventions.* New York: Square Fish, 2014.

Glossary

advertising (AD-vur-tize-ing) the business of promoting things

blizzards (BLIZ-urdz) severe snowstorms with strong winds

briefcase (BREEF-kase) small suitcase for papers that a businessman carries

carriers (KAR-ee-urz) pet containers

dimple (DIM-puhl) a dent in someone's cheek

filters (FIL-turz) devices that remove something unwanted

gags (GAGZ) jokes

gerbils (JUR-buhlz) small, furry animals

manual (MAN-yoo-uhl) a book that gives instructions

offset (awf-SET) to cancel out or make up for

products (PRAH-duhkts) things that are sold

spokes (SPOHKS) thin rods that connect the rim of a wheel to the hub

squinting (SKWINT-ing) partly closing the eyes to see something

Index